RAIN FOREST
MAMMALS

Text and Photography by Edward Parker

RSVP **RAINTREE STECK-VAUGHN PUBLISHERS**

A Harcourt Company

Austin   New York

www.raintreesteckvaughn.com

Copyright Permissions, Steck-Vaughn Company, P.O. Box 26015, Austin, TX 78755.

Published by Raintree Steck-Vaughn Publishers, an imprint of Steck-Vaughn Company

Library of Congress Cataloging-in-Publication data is available upon request.

ISBN 0-7398-5241-8

Printed in Hong Kong. Bound in the United States.

1 2 3 4 5 6 7 8 9 0 LB 07 06 05 04 03

Editor: Sarah Doughty
Design: Bernard Higton
Text consultant: Dr. Paul Toyne

Picture acknowledgments:
All photographs are by Edward Parker with the exception of the following:
OSF 41 top (Konrad Wothe); Still Pictures 8 (Roland Seitre) 9 (Jany Sauvenet), 12 (Klein/Hubert), 13 top (Dominique Halleux), 15 (Roland Seitre), 19 (T. Geer), 20 top & 23 bottom (Norbert Wu), 25 right (Roland Seitre), 26 top (J.J Alcalay), 28 bottom (Gunter Zeisler), 29 top (Daniel Heuclin); WWF-UK 13 & 36 bottom (David Lawson). Artwork is by Peter Bull.

CONTENTS

The Rain Forest Home

Tropical rain forests are home to some of the world's most unusual and secretive mammals. These regions are found near the Equator between the tropics of Cancer and Capricorn. The temperatures here are high and rainfall is greater than 80 inches (2,000 mm) every year. Tropical rain forests are found in South America, in parts of Africa, Southeast Asia, and Australia.

The Amazon region of South America is the largest area of continuous rain forest on earth. In the Amazon rain forest, jaguars prowl the twilight world in search of deer and wild pigs, called peccaries. Tapirs and capybaras move quietly across the ground, plunging into water if they sense

◀ (Above left) Big cats roam through a variety of forests including the rain forests of Asia. The tiger is the largest member of the cat family. Today, there are fewer than 6,000 tigers left in the wild.

▲ (Above right) Rain forests are home to a wide variety of mammals that live in trees. Many species of monkey, such as this titi monkey from the Amazon rain forest, swing through the branches of the rain forest canopy.

NORTH
AMERICA

EUROPE

ASIA

AFRICA

Tropic of Cancer

Equator

SOUTH
AMERICA

Tropic of Capricorn

AUSTRALIA

Original rain forest

Current rain forest

Source: *World Conservation Monitoring Center*

▲ *A map showing the extent of the world's tropical rain forests today, compared with 500 years ago, before large scale deforestation began.*

▼ *Some mammals, such as this tapir, are often found in or near water. When frightened, tapirs plunge into the nearest water and swim away from harm.*

danger. High above the forest floor, chattering monkeys swing and leap through the branches of rain forest trees in search of edible fruits and seeds. In rivers and lakes, dolphins and giant otters surface for air as they search for fish. In the rain forests of Africa, chimpanzees move through the canopy, and rhinos, elephants, and tigers roam the ground. Orangutans and gibbons swing through the branches of rain forests in Southeast Asia. In Australia, unique species of rain forest kangaroos live in trees.

Mammals in the Rain Forest

Mammals share their rain forest home with many species of birds, insects, amphibians, and reptiles. Mammals are the most advanced group of animals on earth. They are warm-blooded and have a bony skeleton. Many have hair or fur on their bodies to keep them warm. Female mammals have special glands called mammary glands that produce milk for feeding their young.

◀ Tropical montane forest in Mexico. This type of forest is home to mammals that can adapt most easily to mountainous conditions.

Lowland Rain Forest and Tropical Montane Forest

There are many different types of tropical rain forests. However, the two most common types are divided according to their height above sea level. These are lowland rain forest and tropical montane forest. Lowland rain forests, such as the Amazon rain forest, contain the majority of rain forest mammal species.

Tropical montane forest occurs on hills and mountains above 3,000 feet (900 m), where conditions are generally cool. Because montane forests are often hidden in dense mists, they are also known as "cloud forests." They are home to their own species of mammals, such as the spectacled bear and the water opossum, both of which live in the mountainous regions of South America.

▼ Spectacled bears are extremely rare and live only in the tropical montane forests of South America.

THE JAGUAR

The jaguar is a cousin of the leopard. It lives in Central and South America, where its habitat extends from Mexico to Argentina. It is the largest carnivore in the Amazon rain forest, up to 8 feet (2.5 m) long, and weighing as much as 300 pounds (140 kg).

The jaguar usually lives in dense areas of rain forest and is an excellent climber. Its favorite food is the peccary, although it will also prey on deer and birds. A powerful swimmer, the jaguar spends large amounts of time near water, waiting to catch fish and turtles. They also attack and eat caimans, which are a type of alligator.

There are fewer jaguars today than in the past. They are sometimes regarded as pests and killed in farming areas if they are a threat to livestock. Jaguars are also hunted illegally for their beautiful spotted skins.

▲ Monkeys are important to the rain forest ecosystem because they help disperse the indigestible seeds of many rain forest plants.

The Importance of Rain Forest Mammals

Mammals are a vital part of the rain forest food chain. Predators such as jaguars and ocelots mainly feed on plant-eating mammals. This helps to control the numbers of animals that eat plants. Other mammals have lifestyles that benefit important plant species in the rain forest. Fruit-eating bats, for example, pollinate plants such as bananas and vanilla flowers. Some mammals are useful because they disperse seeds. Monkeys and tapirs often eat fruit and carry the indigestible seeds in their stomachs for many miles before expelling them from their bodies. The seeds then germinate in a new part of the rain forest.

② THE DIVERSITY OF MAMMALS

The Range of Mammals

Around 65 million years ago, when the dinosaurs died out, mammals started to evolve. The mammals that were the strongest and adapted well to their environment survived, while others died out. Today, there are about five thousand species of mammals. The world's rain forests are estimated to contain around half of all these species. The range of mammals in the rain forest extends from rain forest hippos weighing more than one ton to minute tree shrews weighing less than an ounce.

Although living far apart, some rain forest mammal species have evolved in similar ways. For example, the pangolin of Africa and the tamandua of South America evolved on different continents, but are very similar animals. They are about the same size and shape, and both live in trees and eat only ants.

After millions of years of evolution, many mammals have developed highly specialized lifestyles. Some monkey

▲ The tree shrew is a tiny mammal. It is very similar to the first mammals that existed during the time of the dinosaurs.

◀ The pangolin is sometimes called a scaly anteater. Its diet is made up of ants and its body is covered with flat, bony scales.

OWL MONKEYS

Owl monkeys are a small species that live in the Amazon rain forest. On moonlit nights, owl monkeys search for fruits, seeds, and flower nectar. It is unusual for monkeys to be nocturnal, and it is believed these habits evolved because there is less competition for food at night than during the day.

The monkeys often make long, low calls like a hooting noise as they move around the trees. This helps male and female monkeys locate each other, and makes it easier for young monkeys to find their parents.

Owl monkeys usually rest during the daytime. They sleep in tree hollows, which are generally found amongst the vines and creepers that grow near rivers.

▶ The tamandua is like the pangolin, but has tough hairs on its body instead of bony scales.

species, for example, use their tail like a fifth limb to help them move through the forest. Other species of monkey and sloth have developed special stomachs that allow them to eat poisonous leaves and fruit. Some squirrels have even developed flaps of skin that let them glide from one tree to another.

Secretive Lives

No one knows exactly how many rain forest species exist. Many lead shy and secretive lives, and are rarely seen either by scientists or by local people. Even large mammals, such as the spectacled bear, are well hidden in their mountain habitat. Smaller mammals, such as the numerous species of opossums that inhabit the lowland rain forests of Central and South America, are not only very timid, but often only come out at night.

Number of Mammals

Many of the mammals found in rain forests are small species, such as bats, rats, mice, and porcupines. While rain forests appear to be rich in plants, the vegetation at ground level is sparse because so little light reaches the deep forest floor. This means there is not very much food for the bigger animals to eat. Large mammals that live deep in the forest often have to travel long distances to find enough plant food. Because of this, fewer large mammals per acre live in the rain forest than in other habitats, such as the savannah grasslands of Africa, which have rich and plentiful vegetation.

▲ Rain forests have a wide range of bats, including these flying foxes that live in the mangrove forests of Tanzania in Africa.

RAIN FOREST SECRETS

THE BIGGEST RODENT—THE CAPYBARA

The capybara lives in South America and is the world's biggest rodent. Capybaras are always found near water where they feed

mainly on water plants. When frightened, they plunge into pools or rivers where their webbed feet make them strong swimmers. Above water just their nostrils, eyes, and ears can be seen by predators. Capybaras are prey for jaguars, caimans, and giant snakes called anacondas.

Capybaras are still fairly common in South America where they live in large groups. Their main threat is from humans. People hunt capybaras for their meat and skins and because they destroy crops. In parts of the Amazon rain forest, especially near towns and cities, they have been over-hunted and have almost completely disappeared.

▶ *Pygmy hippos are found in a very small area of the West African rain forest. Because of the lack of food, they are smaller than their relatives in other parts of the world.*

▼ *Many aquatic rain forest mammals are much larger than their relatives from other areas. The world's largest species of otter is found in the Amazon rain forest.*

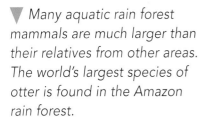

The Size of Rain Forest Species

The scarcity of food has affected the growth of the larger mammals. Many that live deep in the rain forest have evolved into smaller versions of their relatives in other habitats. The pygmy hippo and the royal antelope from the rain forests of West Africa, as well as the Sumatran rhino from Indonesia, are smaller in size than their closest relatives.

However, by contrast, rain forest mammals that live and feed in or near water can grow much larger than their relatives that live in other parts of the world. Rain forest plants are found in abundance along the banks of rivers and have provided plentiful food for mammals such as the capybara. Rivers are a good source of food for aquatic animals. The giant otter is an example of a rain forest mammal that has become larger than its relatives because it has always lived in rivers rich with fish.

Isolated Species

Over millions of years, as continents split apart, rain forests in different parts of the world developed in isolation. In Africa and South America, mammals such as monkeys started to evolve from a common ancestor before the continents separated. However, the continent of Australia was isolated from the rest of the world millions of years before this common ancestor existed. In the rain forests of Australia and Papua New Guinea, other mammals evolved to take the place of these primates. Today, special types of tree kangaroos have similar positions in their ecosystem as monkeys have in other rain forests.

Many species of rain forest monkeys are unique to the continent where they live. Chimpanzees, for example, are only found in the rain forests of West and Central Africa. They developed after the South American continent separated from the African continent, so they are not found in South America. However, South America has about 77 species of primates, and half of these are only found in the Amazon rain forest. Some species of primates are even more localized. The golden lion tamarin, for example, is found in just a few thousand acres of Atlantic forest on the coast of Brazil.

▲ This tree kangaroo lives in Papua New Guinea. It is an example of an animal that has evolved to live in the trees, much as monkeys do in other parts of the world.

RAIN FOREST SECRETS

LEMURS—THE INDRI

The rain forest on the island of Madagascar is inhabited by many unusual species of mammals. Among these are lemurs, which are often described as "primitive monkeys." Lemurs are descended from the same ancient ancestor as monkeys and apes. Over millions of years they have evolved into a large variety of species. The pygmy mouse lemur, for example, is so small that it could sit in a small paper cup. The largest lemur, the indri (right), grows to over 3 feet (1 m) long and weighs around 15 pounds (7 kg).

Humans first arrived in Madagascar around 1,200 years ago. Lemurs were killed for food and parts of their habitat were gradually destroyed. Over hundreds of years, 15 species became extinct. There are now only about 50 species of lemur left.

The giant island of Madagascar, which lies to the southeast of Africa, split away from the African continent 150 million years ago. Monkeys did not evolve on this island in the same way as in other rain forests. Instead, different types of lemur evolved. Lemurs have long, slender bodies, long tails, and thick, woolly fur. However, their lives are similar to monkeys found elsewhere.

◀ *Chimpanzees belong to a group of intelligent monkeys called apes. They evolved after the continents of Africa and South America separated and are only found in Africa.*

Different Rain Forest Habitats

Rain forests in different parts of the world often look quite similar, but each has unique conditions and combinations of plant and animal species.

The most widespread type of rain forest is lowland rain forest, such as the Amazon. The two main main types of lowland forest are the *terra firme* (dry ground forest) and the *várzea* (flooded forest). In the *várzea*, parts of the rain forest are submerged for several months of the year, leaving only the tallest trees visible. Another important type of lowland rain forest is the mangrove forest found along coastal areas.

Most mammals have adapted to particular types of forest, but some mammals can live in a variety of habitats. Pumas, for example, can thrive in most parts of both the lowland rain forest and the tropical montane forest that occurs on the upper slopes of hills and mountains.

▲ *A typical interior of lowland rain forest near Belém in Brazil. The lowland areas of the Amazon rain forest are home to mammal species such as tapirs, jaguars, and ocelots.*

SLOTHS—LIFE IN THE CANOPY

The sloth spends most of its life hanging upside down in a tree. Sloths have adapted to a sluggish pace of life, moving through branches at a rate of one half mile (one kilometer) per hour, and eating leaves that most other mammals cannot digest. The sloth also has special hairs that have grooves for algae to grow in. This helps camouflage the sloth as it moves slowly through the vegetation of the canopy.

Although a sloth cannot walk well, it is perfectly adapted to hanging upside down suspended on long, slender claws. It is so effortless for a sloth to hang upside down that when a sloth dies it remains hanging while it decomposes.

▲ Red colobus monkeys have specially adapted stomachs so they can eat leaves from the canopy.

▼ Giant anteaters are found on the floor of dry ground forest in the Amazon.

Fascinating Fact

The sloth has one of the smallest mammal brains—about the size of a marble.

Levels of Lowland Rain Forest

Rain forest mammals are adapted to life at different levels within a lowland rain forest. Some species of mammals, such as monkeys, sloths, and bats, spend most of their lives high up in the canopy. Others, such as various types of deer and anteaters, forage on the rain forest floor for plants or insects to eat. Tapirs, capybara, giant otters, and jaguars spend much of their time searching for fish and other river prey.

◀ Terra firme *forest in the Amazon is characterized by large trees which can grow to heights of over 230 feet (70 m). Dry ground forest provides habitats for both ground and tree-living mammals.*

Lowland Amazonian Rain Forest

In the Amazon rain forest, most mammals live in the *terra firme* forest. Large herds of white-lipped peccaries can be found here along with mammals such as anteaters and coatimundis. Many of the mammals that live in dry ground forest cannot get across rivers. Some species of marmoset are believed to have been isolated on "islands" of dry land between rivers for tens of thousands of years.

The *terra firme* forests also have species of trees and plants not found elsewhere. Many species of mammals survive on very specific types of fruits, seeds, and leaves. Bats and monkeys often rely on the fruits and flower nectar from a limited number of tree species, and usually have to travel large distances between trees to find food.

▲ *The coatimundi is a type of raccoon that spends time both climbing among the trees and foraging for food on the ground in Central and South American rain forests.*

▲ *A typical view of the flooded forest of the upper Amazon as the waters begin to rise at the start of the wet season.*

Flooded Forest

Flooded areas occur in rain forests around the world, but the largest and most famous is the flooded forest in the upper Amazon near the Brazilian city of Manaus. Here the water levels fall and rise by as much as 40 feet (13 m) between the dry and wet seasons. The types of trees that can survive this flooding are very different from those that are found in the dry ground forest. Many mammals that live in these trees, such as sloths and squirrel monkeys, move out of the rain forest when it becomes flooded. Other species, such as the uakari monkey, have adapted to living in the flooded forest all year round and only come down to the ground in the dry season. Species such as dolphins and manatees swim between the branches of the submerged trees in search of food during the flooded season.

RAIN FOREST SECRETS

THE UAKARI MONKEY

The white uakari is found only in untouched areas of the flooded forest east of the Amazon city of Manaus. It is a medium-sized monkey weighing between 4 and 9 pounds (2 and 4 kg). A white uakari is very distinctive, with a shaggy white coat, a short bushy tail, and a spectacular red face.

Uakari monkeys spend most of their time in the canopy of the flooded forest. During the dry season they come down to ground level and search out seeds and fallen fruit. They have specially adapted teeth that allow them to open the husks of unripe fruits and seeds, and a special stomach to cope with the toxic chemicals used by plants to protect unripe seeds.

THE SPECTACLED BEAR

Mangrove Forest

Mangrove forest covers a much smaller area than *terra firme* forest—an area of about 900 square miles (2,400 sq km). Coastal mangrove forests are frequently visited by mammals such as dolphins and manatees. Some types of vervet monkeys visit the forest along the Indian Ocean coastline of Africa in search of crabs, shellfish, fruit, and seeds. In other parts of the world, mammals such as the crab-eating raccoon also hunt and scavenge among the bell-shaped roots of mangrove trees.

The spectacled bear is South America's only species of bear. It lives mainly in the tropical montane forest at the foothills of the Andes, although it occasionally visits lowland rain forests.

Spectacled bears eat fruits, nuts, insects, and leaves. One of their favorite foods are bromeliads (see above right), which are plants that grow on the branches of trees. Bears like to climb up and eat the fleshy centers.

Each spectacled bear requires over 2 square miles (6 sq km) of undisturbed tropical montane forest for its survival. Spectacled bears are now very rare because large areas of forest have been destroyed or disturbed.

◀ *Mangrove forests are not home to many species of mammals, although they are frequently visited.*

▲ Mountain gorillas are among the world's rarest mammals. They live in tropical montane forest in central African countries such as Rwanda, where they feed mainly on fruits and leaves.

Tropical Montane Forest

There are many species of mammals that live in tropical montane forest. The plants that grow on the branches and trunks of montane forest trees, such as orchids and bromeliads, are a source of food for particular types of bats, opossums, spiny tree rats, and spectacled bears. Because of the cooler temperatures that exist in these forests, montane mammals often have thicker fur than those living in lowland rain forests. Tropical montane forest is home to the mountain gorilla, which is found only in very restricted areas in central Africa.

4 LIFESTYLES

Living in the Rain Forest

The lifestyle of mammals depends on the part of the rain forest they live in and the food they eat. Monkeys, for example, are well adapted to living in the canopy. They use their strong hands for gripping and their tail for balance as they move quickly through the branches in search of fruit, nuts, and leaves. They can reach the emergent layers of the rain forest at a height of about 230 feet (70 m) above the canopy.

Other mammals are better adapted to living in the twilight world of the rain forest floor. Deer and tapirs feed on plants, armadillos search for insects, and agoutis find nuts and seeds on the ground. Leopards roam the rain forest floor, but they are also excellent climbers and often lie among the tree branches, silently waiting to ambush their prey. Aquatic mammals, such as dolphins and manatees, are well adapted to life in the water of lowland rain forests.

▲ Armadillos are common to the rain forests of South and Central America, where they feed mainly on a diet of insects.

▼ The Brazilian bare-faced tamarin thrives in the dense vegetation of the rain forest and is found mainly along river banks.

RAIN FOREST SECRETS

A MERMAID MYTH

The manatee is an aquatic mammal that is similar to a large seal. Manatees live in lowland rivers and along mangrove coasts.

The Senegal manatees of West Africa are believed to have inspired stories about mermaids. Mermaids are mythical creatures, half women and half fish. Sailors who saw manatees from a distance, cradling their young in their flippers, mistook them for mermaids breast-feeding their babies.

Manatees were once common in the Amazon but they are now very rare. One species of manatee has already been hunted to extinction. In West Africa, fishermen set traps to catch manatees as they move into the mangrove swamps when the tide rises.

Groups of Mammals

Mammals are often divided into groups that have similar lifestyles or distinctive features. For example, rodents such as rats, mice, and squirrels form a distinct group because of their canine teeth. Aquatic mammals form another group. Animals that are carnivores, such as cats and raccoons, make up a group of meat eaters, while herbivores, such as deer and elephants, make up a group of plant eaters. Omnivores are a group that eat a variety of food. They include primates such as apes and monkeys. Bats make up a group of their own because they are the only mammals that can fly.

◀ *The green agouti is a rodent that feeds on nuts and seeds. It uses its sharp teeth and strong jaw muscles to break open tough shells.*

◀ *The jaguar is the most fierce carnivore in the lowland forests of South and Central America. Like other carnivores, it has large canine teeth to tear the flesh of its victim.*

Fascinating Fact

The jaguar spends a great deal of its time near water. It sometimes lures fish by dangling its tail in the water and scooping them up with its huge paws.

Cats

Six species of cat live in the rain forests of South and Central America. In the Amazon rain forest, cats are the main predators. They use their canine teeth for killing and tearing the flesh of prey. They also have sharp claws and powerful shoulders, and are capable of bringing down and killing large animals. Most types of cats, such as jaguars and margays, are solitary hunters and capture prey by moving stealthily through the undergrowth. The spots of cats such as the ocelot, margay, and jaguar help camouflage them in the dappled light of the rain forest floor.

THE PUMA

The puma is the most wide ranging and successful cat species in the Americas. Pumas are able to thrive in any habitat where there are plenty of animals such as deer, agoutis, and pacas to eat.

Pumas are found throughout both lowland rain forest and tropical montane forest, but prefer dry ground where possible. They are equally well suited to many other types of environment, and can be found as far north as Canada and as far south as the tip of Chile.

Raccoons and Weasels

The mammals that are part of the raccoon family live in Central and South America. These include the coatimundi, the crab-eating raccoon, and the kinkajou, which is similar to the raccoon. Raccoons are mainly omnivores and eat insects, crabs, frogs, and snakes as well as fruits and seeds. Members of the raccoon family are all good tree climbers and can also feed on nesting birds.

There are eight species of mammal that make up the weasel family. They include skunks and otters. Members of the weasel family are very aggressive and can kill and eat prey much larger than themselves.

Several species of otter live along the rivers of lowland rain forest in the Amazon and also thrive in the fast-flowing rivers and streams of tropical montane forest in South America.

▼ *The kinkajou is a type of raccoon that lives in the rain forests of South and Central America.*

Elephants

In Africa, there are certain types of elephant that live only in the rain forest. They are a subspecies of the African elephant and are generally much smaller than elephants that live on the savannah. Little is known about them because they lead secretive lives in some of the most inaccessible rain forest in the Congo basin. The Asian elephant, sometimes called the Indian elephant, is also a rain forest plant eater, but few Asian elephants remain in the wild because they have been hunted and their habitat destroyed.

◀ Asian elephants used to live in large numbers throughout the rainforests of Asia, but today there are only a few herds left. They usually feed on shoots, leaves, and fruit.

▼ Congo rain forest cattle live in the world's second largest area of rain forest, which covers the Congo river basin in Africa.

Deer and Cattle

Deer are also rain forest plant eaters. Deer originated in Asia and have only recently—about 12,000 years ago—crossed the Bering Strait into the Americas from Russia. Deer are common in Asia, where many species live, although in the South American rain forest only three species exist today.

Rain forest cattle do not exist in the wild in South or Central America and are found only in Africa and Asia. These mammals are typically smaller than domestic cattle. Today, large areas of rain forest land in the Amazon is used for herding domestic cattle.

THE LOWLAND TAPIR

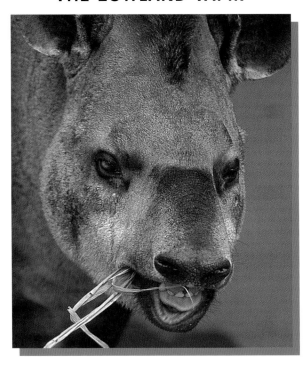

The largest plant eater that lives on dry land in the Amazon rain forest is the lowland tapir which can weigh up to 550 pounds (250 kg). It is an unusual animal, related to both the horse and the rhino, that have similar three-toed feet. Like horses and rhinos, tapirs have special stomachs where plant material is broken down into digestible material. They have a short, prehensile upper lip that can reach out and pull leaves toward their mouth.

The lowland tapirs are mostly nocturnal and feed mainly on swamp plants, grass, and fruits. They spend most of their time near the water, although they can also negotiate steep mountainsides and dry forest floors. When startled, they plunge into water and can swim quite long distances under the surface.

Peccaries

Peccaries are mainly plant eaters, despite their long, downward pointing canine teeth. However, like most species of pig, they are omnivorous because they will eat insects and even small mammals on occasion. Their canine teeth are enlarged for defense as well as combat with other peccaries.

▲ Collared peccaries live in small family groups of about six to nine individuals.

White-lipped peccaries move in large herds of 50–300 individuals for safety against predators. Collared peccaries, by contrast, live fairly solitary lives in small family groups. To avoid being heard by predators, small groups of collared peccaries move silently through the rain forest.

Fascinating Fact

Peccaries have such poor eyesight that they will walk right up to a person who is standing still.

Large Primates

Large primates, such as chimpanzees and gorillas, are found in Africa, while orangutans and gibbons live in Southeast Asia. Because the rain forests of South America do not contain large apes, large monkeys have evolved to fill similar positions in their ecosystems.

Large Monkeys

Large monkeys include spider, woolly, and howler monkeys, all of which weigh more than 9 pounds (4 kg) when fully grown. They mainly eat fruits and leaves. Large monkeys reproduce very slowly. Female woolly monkeys, for example, first give birth when they are between six and eight years old, and then produce just one baby every other year.

Medium Sized Monkeys

Medium sized monkeys, including the sakis, uakaris, and capuchin monkeys, are found in the Amazon, and weigh between 4 and 9 pounds (2 and 4 kg). They have large lower canine teeth that are used to split open the husks of unripe fruit and nuts. Capuchin monkeys often forage in groups of five to twenty, eating seeds, fruits, insects, eggs, lizards, and even small mammals such as opossums.

▲ Orangutans are the second largest apes in the world. They are superb tree climbers at all levels of the rain forest.

◀ The brown capuchin monkey eats a more varied diet than many other species of monkey.

Fascinating Fact

Colobus monkeys have special stomachs that allow them to eat fruits and seeds which are deadly poisonous to other animals.

RAIN FOREST SECRETS

PREHENSILE TAILS

Some species of monkey in South and Central America have developed a prehensile tail that they use as a "fifth limb." Woolly monkeys (see right) and spider monkeys can use their tails for extra balance or to hang upside down, allowing them to use both hands and feet while feeding. It also lets them spread their weight better on branches and find food that would otherwise be out of reach.

In the Amazon rain forest, several other types of mammals have developed prehensile tails, including the tree tamandua (also known as the tree anteater), the carnivorous kinkajou, and several species of opossum.

▼ *A pygmy marmoset holding the tail of a partly eaten lizard.*

Small Monkeys

In the Amazon rain forest, there are numerous small monkeys. The smallest primates are the marmosets and tamarins, including the pygmy marmoset that weighs just 3.5 ounces (100 g). Marmosets and tamarins both feed extensively on plant sap and have special, sharp canine teeth for gouging holes in tree trunks. Small monkeys include the squirrel and titi monkeys, which are very agile and scamper along the branches searching for seeds, fruits, insects, and leaves. Squirrel monkeys live in large groups in the middle levels of the rain forest. They often have their homes near rivers, where there are plenty of branches and vines.

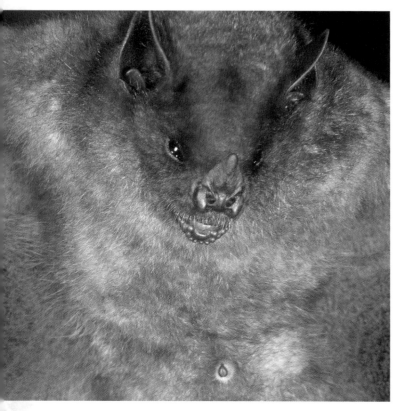

▲ Many bats, such as this one from the tropical montane forest in Ecuador, eat only fruit.

Bats

Bats are the only mammals that can fly. They are the second largest group of mammals, after rodents, with 950 species worldwide. In the rain forests of Central America, there are more bat species than all other mammal species combined.

Bats are able to fly because their arms and fingers are covered in a remarkable thin, rubbery skin that forms wings. In the rain forests of South America, all the species of bats use sound to help them fly at night and locate food. The bats make a high clicking sound that humans cannot hear.

RAIN FOREST SECRETS

VAMPIRE BATS

There are three species of vampire bats in the rain forests of South and Central America. These bats feed on the blood of birds and mammals, including the blood of humans on occasion. They hunt at night and attack their victims as they sleep. Vampire bats use their razor sharp teeth to make a quick and painless wound. They do not suck blood from the body but lick it up with their tongues as it flows from the wound. Vampire bats have a special substance in their saliva that stops the blood from clotting until the bat has finished feeding.

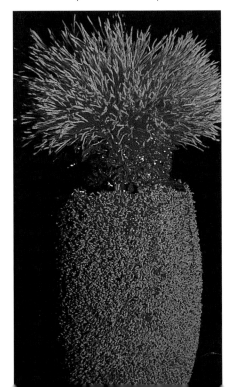

▼ *The shape of the parkia flower, found in West Africa, makes it easy for bats to feed from it and, therefore, pollinate the plant.*

▲ *This Geoffroy's long-nosed bat from the rain forests of French Guiana in South America is feeding on nectar and taking pollen from a flower. Many species of bat pollinate rain forest plants.*

By listening to the echoes of these sounds, they can judge where objects are in total darkness. This is called echolocation.

Bats are extremely well adapted to life in the rain forest. During the day they normally sleep together in big groups, hanging upside down with their wings folded. At night they wake up to feed. Bats usually eat fruit, insects, and the nectar from flowers. As they feed on the nectar, the tip of their tongue takes up pollen along with the nectar and pollinates the flower. Bats are also important in spreading seeds. When they eat fruit, such as figs, the seeds get passed through their bodies and are deposited as waste. In this way, the seeds are spread throughout the rain forest.

⑤ DISAPPEARING MAMMALS

Why are Mammals Disappearing?

The number of many rain forest mammal species has declined rapidly over the last thirty years. Mammals such as mountain gorillas, spectacled bears, tigers, rhinos, manatees, and orangutans have declined so drastically that they are in danger of becoming extinct. The number of golden lion tamarins in Brazil's Atlantic forest, for example, fell to a few hundred individuals in the 1990s, and there are now less than 800 mountain gorillas left in Africa.

There are many reasons why some rain forest mammals are disappearing. However, the largest single cause is the destruction of their habitat.

◀ A large tree is felled in the rain forest of Cameroon in West Africa. Logging in West Africa is causing the destruction of many rain forest habitats.

◀ Millions of people in Africa eat "bush meat." Bush meat can be any sort of meat from wild mammals, and includes meat from monkeys, deer, manatees, and large rodents.

LINKS

Medicines and Charms

The organs of particular rain forest mammals are believed by many people to have special magical or medicinal properties. In India and a number of other Asian countries, for example, the gall bladder of a sloth bear is reputed to cure liver and stomach problems. Thousands of these wild animals are killed in order to use their organs for such purposes.

In the Amazon and Andes mountains, parts of jaguars and spectacled bears are sold as medicines or as charms.

▼ Small monkeys such as this squirrel monkey are popular as pets and many are taken from the wild to supply the pet trade.

Large carnivores are also shot because of the risk that they will kill someone or eat livestock. They are hunted for food, for their skins, and for their internal organs, which are believed to have medicinal properties.

The Pet Trade

Tens of thousands of rain forest mammals, such as small monkeys, are trapped and sold as pets. It is also common for the parents of mammals such as orangutans to be killed so their young can be sold to people who live in nearby towns or cities. Sometimes they are sold abroad. In the Amazon region, monkeys such as squirrel monkeys and capuchins are regularly kept as house pets. In the Indian subcontinent, some species of bear are captured and made to dance to earn money for their owners.

◀ A jaguar being skinned in an Amazonian village. The meat will be eaten and the skin sold.

▼ A young boy with a monkey which has been killed for food in Cameroon.

Hunting

Rain forest mammals have been hunted for more than a million years to provide food for people. The very first people to move into the rain forest are believed to have been hunters. Until recently, the number of inhabitants living in the rain forests was very low. Today, there are more than 150 million people living in, or close to, the rain forests. Hunting is having a serious effect on mammals. Animals are not only hunted for food; many rare animals are also killed by professional hunters for sport. In parts of Africa, there is a large trade in bush meat from animals such as deer and monkeys. In the Amazon, as elsewhere, manatees are hunted for their meat. One species of manatee has already become extinct, and the three remaining species are endangered.

Skin Trade

The hunting of animals for their skins is another human activity that is causing mammal numbers to decline in rain forests. Tigers, jaguars, and ocelots have been hunted heavily because their beautiful skins can be sold for large sums of money. The killing continues even though it is often illegal. For poor people in the rain forest, selling skins is one way to earn money to feed their families. On a bigger scale, criminal organizations often smuggle skins to wealthy buyers in the rich countries of the world.

▼ *A peccary skin is dried on a frame before being sold in a local Amazonian town.*

HUNTING THE GIANT OTTER

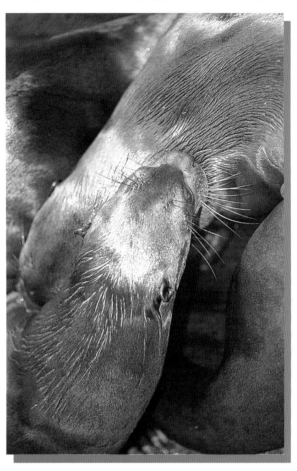

In the Amazon, the giant otter has suffered at the hands of people. Otters have been heavily hunted both for their skins and because they compete with people for fish in rivers. One of the reasons why giant otters have suffered so badly is that they are accessible to hunters. Otters live on river banks where they cannot hide. The sound of giant otters noisily squeaking and surfacing with loud snorts makes them easy targets for hunters.

Disappearing Habitats

The most serious threat to rain forest mammals is the loss of their homes. When rain forests are cut down or burned, it can take hundreds of years for them to recover. Without the insects and plants that they need to survive, many mammals must move away or risk dying of hunger.

As rain forests are destroyed, mammals are forced to live in smaller and smaller areas. Some types of rain forests have been so seriously affected that they are in danger of disappearing entirely, along with the animals that live in them. The Atlantic forest in Brazil, for example, has been reduced to just 5 percent of its original area, and the same is true of the rain forests of Madagascar, which are considered to be the most threatened rain forests in the world.

Fascinating Fact

There are now believed to be less than 400 Sumatran rhinos left in the wild.

◄ *Drilling for oil and the construction of long pipelines across the Amazon rain forest is having a major impact on mammal populations.*

Human Activities

Human activities play a large part in rain forest destruction. Huge areas are being cut down to produce timber, firewood, charcoal, and wood pulp for paper. Other large areas are being converted into agricultural land.

LINKS

Burning the Rain forest

Every year in the Amazon, burning destroys thousands of square miles of rain forest. The fires are so regular that September is often called the *quemada*, or the burning season. Rain forest fires kill many mammals. Sloths, for example, cannot move away from danger quickly enough. Many species of primates cannot get across rivers and streams to escape. Armadillos are vulnerable because they simply roll up into a tight ball when frightened. Young deer die because their parents usually leave them hidden in the undergrowth while they search for food.

Soy bean production in the Amazon and palm oil plantations in Africa and Asia have caused the loss of millions of square miles of rain forest. Building dams, digging mines, and the expansion of towns and cities have also led to rain forest loss.

▶ *Thousands of square miles of rain forest in the Amazon have been destroyed to make way for cattle ranching. This area of rain forest is in Acre State, Brazil.*

⑥ CONSERVATION

◄ Many environmental organizations are campaigning to save the remaining habitat of the orangutan.

▼ Tigers are now very rare. It is believed that there are only a few thousand left in India. To help protect tigers, the government has made it illegal to hunt them or sell their skins.

Saving the Species

The number of rare mammals such as tigers, orangutans, and manatees is so low that urgent action is needed if they are to survive even the next twenty years. Fortunately, there are many excellent organizations highlighting their plight and working hard to conserve species of mammals. Many rain forest communities have their own rules and ways of living that help ensure the survival of rare species.

The successful protection and conservation of rare rain forest mammal species is not easy, but there are a variety of ways in which people are trying to help. Organizations such as WWF and Friends of the Earth (FOE) campaign for the protection of rain forests and for a better balance between the needs of wildlife, rain forest people, and businesses who wish to develop the rain forests.

LINKS

Research in Madagascar

In Madagascar, 95 percent of the rain forest has been destroyed. Scientists are now carrying out research into how quickly certain types of mammals can return to an area, after it has been burned. The researchers hope to understand which animals can adapt to a renewed forest most easily. They also want to discover if there are ways of speeding up the regeneration of the rain forests to help the mammals.

In order to undertake research, scientists have to set traps to catch rain forest mammals. They are caught by pit traps (see far right) where a plastic barrier guides the mammals towards a container where they are caught and collected. The animals are weighed and measured (see right) before being released with an identification tag.

Research

The role of researchers in conservation is an important one. Scientists carry out research to estimate the numbers of rare animals and to study how particular mammals live. Some rare species rely on certain types of food and special habitats. The spectacled bear, for example, needs to reach the bromeliads that grow on the branches of trees. Scientists have found that the bears cannot live in areas that have been replanted recently because the young trees are too weak for bears to climb up and reach their food.

Protected Areas

One of the ways to help rare mammals survive is by protecting the rain forests in which they live. If the areas are big enough, even large mammals such as rhinos, tigers, and elephants can be given a good chance of survival. WWF and other organizations have successfully campaigned for protected areas to be set up all over the world. These can take the form of national parks, nature reserves, community managed land, forest reserves, and rain forest linking larger areas of rain forest.

There have been many campaigns for the protection of some of the most popular rain forest species. As a result, there are special parks for animals such as jaguars, lemurs, and rhinos. Many campaigns focus on the best-known and most "appealing" species as a means of getting an area protected. This also helps less "appealing" mammals, such as bats or anteaters, which also benefit whenever an area of rain forest becomes protected.

▲ Indigenous people play an important part in conservation. This area of tropical montane forest in southern Mexico is owned, managed, and protected by local Zapotec people.

▼ In 1984, the Cockscomb Wildlife Sanctuary was established for the protection of jaguars in the Central American country of Belize.

International Law

Over the last few decades, wildlife has been given much more protection by the introduction of new laws. In many countries, there are national laws that aim to stop the hunting of rare mammals. International laws prevent skins, ivory, and other rare animal products from being traded around the world. Under the United Nation's Convention on Biological Diversity, countries agree to help protect rare species from becoming extinct.

▲ *The Udzungwa Mountain Forest in Tanzania is a national park that provides a home to some of Africa's rarest species of monkey.*

LINKS

Laws against International Trade

The Convention in the Trade of Endangered Species of flora and fauna (CITES) is an international law preventing trade in rare species of plants and animals.

This law has been effective in reducing the trade in rare animal skins, such as these ocelot skins (see right). There used to be a major trade in skins of rare mammals such as tigers, jaguars, and giant otters.

Today, some attempts are made to smuggle skins from these mammals, but customs officers at major international airports search passengers and cargo for illegal animal products.

Squirrel monkeys are one of the small primates that benefit from disturbances in the rain forest caused by small scale agriculture.

Rain forest that is recolonized after being deforested provides ideal conditions for the emperor tamarin. It likes to climb on the trunks of the new, small trees that grow close to one another.

Sharing the Rain Forest

For the descendants of people who have lived in the rain forest for thousands of years, sharing the rain forest with animals is a natural way of life. However, there are people who have migrated to the rain forest because they have nowhere else to live. Some of them may use the rain forest in a wasteful or destructive way. Destroying the rain forest on a local scale can affect both communities and wildlife. Organizations such as WWF recognize that people have to make a living so they support projects and communities that use the rain forest in a way that benefits both the people and the animals. Small scale agriculture can actually help the rain forest. In Brazil, it was discovered that small primates, such as marmosets, thrive where people cut down small patches of rain forest. The young trees that recolonize these cut areas provide a suitable habitat and an important source of food for these small primates.

DOLPHINS

In the rivers and lakes of the Amazon rain forest there are two types of dolphin—the pink river dolphin and the grey dolphin. Pink river dolphins (see right) eat between 9 and 11 pounds (4 and 5 kg) of fish a day, and are often in direct competition with local fishermen. Despite this, indigenous rain forest people do not usually hunt these mammals. This is mainly due to the myths and stories that surround dolphins. In some areas of the Amazon, people believe that dolphins can walk on land at night as humans. In other areas, dolphins are linked to the powerful spirit of the moon.

▼ Small primates can thrive in areas where the rain forest has been cut down and recolonized.

Maintaining Populations

In traditional rain forest communities there are often rules that help maintain mammal populations. In the Amazon, for example, indigenous hunters will not kill an animal if it is with its young. They also have rules about how many animals can be killed.

Traditional beliefs have also helped to maintain mammal populations. In the Andes, many indigenous communities do not hunt spectacled bears because they believe these bears communicate with the gods who live in the dense clouds at the top of the mountains. In the Amazon, many indigenous groups have beliefs about dolphins that save these mammals from being hunted.

Zoos and Conservation

Zoos are important centers for studying the behavior of animals, since it is much easier to learn about them in captivity. Zoos and other scientific research centers also have an important role in the conservation of rain forest mammals. Some wild animals, such as the buffy-headed capuchin monkeys from Brazil, and the mountain gorillas of Rwanda, are so rare that, without help, they will become extinct. Modern zoos not only have some rain forest animals for the public to see, but they are also trying to increase animal numbers in the wild. To do this, the animals are bred in captivity.

▲ *Children learning about a conservation project from a display at Chester Zoo in England.*

LINKS

Conservation in Action

Like many major zoos worldwide, Chester Zoo in northwest England runs a number of conservation projects aimed at increasing the understanding of animals in the wild.

Since 1996, Chester Zoo has been helping to breed the rare buffy-headed capuchin monkey from the Atlantic forest (see below). It has also successfully bred orangutans.

In 2000, Chester Zoo signed an agreement with Chengdu Zoo in China to collaborate on research into the endangered panda.

► *A scientist in the Atlantic rain forest of Brazil uses tracking equipment to locate a young golden lion tamarin that has a fitted radio collar. This enables scientists to follow and study groups of tamarins in dense rain forest.*

Fascinating Fact

Since 1972, a campaign run by WWF called Project Tiger has led to the setting up of 23 special reserves to help conserve tigers.

The young are then released into protected areas to increase the wild populations. Often, the zookeepers have to teach the young animals how to live and survive away from captivity. Scientists may use tracking devices in order to locate and follow the animals they have released.

Supporting Environment Organizations

Campaigns are run by organizations such as the WWF to highlight the plight of animals such as tigers, gorillas, and jaguars. These organizations also fund conservation activities around the world and champion laws to stop the trade in rare animal products. Joining and supporting environmental organizations is one way that people who live far away from rain forests can help protect and conserve rain forest mammals.

Increasing Destruction

The Amazon rain forest is currently undergoing large scale logging and the clearance of land for ranching and agriculture. The rate of destruction is showing no signs of slowing down. The world's growing population puts great demands on rain forest resources. Rain forests often exist in the world's poorest countries, and governments often have little option but to exploit their resources to earn the money needed for development and repaying the debts they may owe to richer countries.

Rain forests such as the Amazon need sustainable development which meets the needs of local people as well as conservation. There are economic activities that can be undertaken in rain forests that can both provide people with a living and protect the rain forests.

▲ An area of flooded forest in the Amazon that is protected. This benefits monkeys like the uakari and aquatic mammals such as dolphins, manatees, and otters.

▼ Ecotourism is being encouraged as a way of helping the rain forests. This walkway in a tourist area near Manaus helps people locate the animals.

Developing Ecotourism

Many tourists are willing to take vacations to see rare mammals in rain forest areas. Ecotourism is a growing industry that preserves the rain forest and the species that live in them. It is also a way of providing income for local people. They can earn more money through tourism than through activities such as hunting mammals, selling skins, deforestation, and growing crops.

RAIN FOREST SECRETS

GOLDEN LION TAMARIN

In early 2001, a landmark event took place in a small part of Brazil's Atlantic forest. The number of one of the world's rarest primates, the golden lion tamarin, had exceeded 1,000 individuals for the first time in many years. Zoos from all over the world and environmental organizations such as WWF had been working for twenty years to stop this small primate from becoming extinct. Young tamarins bred in zoos were released into the wild and nesting boxes for them were provided. Local farmers made parts of their land into sanctuaries for the monkeys. Eventually, the decline in numbers was halted.

This success proves that if we take action we can save many of the world's endangered species from becoming extinct.

▼ *Several new species of woolly monkey similar to this were found in the Amazon rain forest in 2000.*

The Future

The future of many rain forest mammals is uncertain. With the current rate of rain forest destruction, there is a real possibility that eventually many rare species may exist only in parks and zoos. It is only by protecting rain forests and undertaking conservation programs that the future for mammals can look brighter. It is up to all of us to ensure that rain forest wildlife has a better future.

Fascinating Fact

At least eight new species of monkey have been discovered in the Amazon rain forest since 1999.

GLOSSARY

Orangutan.

ape A large monkey-like mammal such as a gorilla, chimpanzee, orangutan, or gibbon. Unlike a monkey, an ape has no tail.

aquatic An animal or plant that lives in or near water.

bromeliads A group of plants that come from the Americas and have a rosette of spiny leaves.

camouflage Colors, shapes, or patterns that help an animal blend in with its surroundings.

canine A large tooth near the front of the mouth.

canopy The layer of trees between the rain forest floor and the tallest towering treetops.

captivity Being kept in a particular area, held in by a cage or fence.

conservation Looking after the environment and its resources.

ecosystem A community of different species and the environment they live in.

ecotourism Activities where tourists visit natural environments with an interest in conserving them.

emergents Tall trees that tower above the canopy, often with a cauliflower-shaped crown.

endangered When a species is at risk of dying out.

epiphytes Plants that grow on other plants.

evolve When a species of any living organism develops naturally over many generations.

extinct When a species of any living organism, such as an animal or plant, no longer exists.

food chain A series of organisms in a habitat. Each one is dependent on the next for food.

habitat The natural home of a particular plant or animal.

mammary glands Special organs that are unique to female mammals and produce milk for their young.

mangroves A swamp forest found on tropical and subtropical tidal mud flats.

national parks Parks that are recognized by national governments as important areas for conservation.

nature reserves Areas of land that are set up for the protection of wildlife.

pollinate To transfer pollen from the male to the female parts of a flower.

predators Animals that naturally prey on other animals.

prehensile Part of an animal's body that can grab or act like a limb.

prey An animal that is hunted and killed by another for food.

primates Highly evolved species of mammals that include lemurs, monkeys, apes, and humans.

sap The vital liquid that circulates inside plants.

savannah Open grasslands in tropical or subtropical areas. Few bushes or trees grow in these habitats.

species A group of animals or plants that are similar to one another and can breed together.

FURTHER INFORMATION

BOOKS TO READ

Chinery, Michael. *Predators and Prey: Secrets of the Rainforest.* New York: Crabtree, 2000.

George, Jean Craighead. *One Day in the Tropical Rainforest.* New York: HarperCollins, 1995.

Greenaway, Theresa. *Jungle.* New York: Dorling Kindersley Publishing, 2000.

Harris, Nicholas. *Into the Rainforest: One Book Makes Hundreds of Pictures of Rain Forest Life (The Ecosystems Xplorer).* New York: Time Life, 1996.

Knight, Tim. *Journey into the Rainforest.* New York: Oxford University Press, 2001.

Lasky, Kathryn. *The Most Beautiful Roof in the World: Exploring the Rain Forest Canopy.* Reading, MA: Scott Foresman, 1997.

Lewington, Anna. *Antonio's Rainforest.* Minneapolis, MN: The Lerner Publishing Group, 1996.

Sauvain, Philip. *Geography Detective: Rainforests.* Minneapolis, MN: Carolrhoda Books, Inc., 1997.

Wood, Selina. *The Rainforest.* Brookfield, CT: Millbrook Press, 1997.

Young, Allen M. *Tropical Rainforests: 230 Species in Full Color.* New York: Griffin Trade Paperback, 2001.

VIDEO

National Geographic's Really Wild Animals: Totally Tropical Rain Forest, National Geographic Video, 1994.

ADDRESSES OF ORGANIZATIONS

Friends of the Earth
1025 Vermont Avenue, N.W., Suite 300
Washington, D.C. 20005-6303
Tel: 202-783-7400
Web site: www.foe.org

Greenpeace
702 H Street, N.W.
Washington, D.C. 20001
Tel: 1-800-326-0959
Web site: www.greenpeaceusa.org

Oxfam America
1112 16th Street, N.W., Suite 600
Washington, D.C. 20036
Tel: 202-496-1180
Web site: www.oxfamamerica.org

World Wildlife Fund
1250 24th Street, N.W.
Washington, D.C. 20037
Tel: 202-293-4800
Web site: www.worldwildlife.org

INDEX